ANDREW CAYMAN

OPTIONS AND

DAY TRADING:

Everything You Need To Know To Make Money
Online. Start Investing In Options, Stocks And
Futures Like An Expert Trader.

© Copyright 2020 - All rights reserved.

Table of Contents

Introduction

There are a lot of benefits with day trading. Everyone can profit from this kind of trading, as long as they are willing to take some time to look through the trends and charts and make sound decisions. You also need to be willing to leave your emotions at the door. While day trading can be profitable and a lot of fun, many times, it can be challenging and emotional as well, especially if a trade starts to go against what you were hoping to see.

There are a ton of securities and stocks on the market that you can choose from. It provides you with many opportunities to enter the market and provides you with some freedom when it comes to seeing results. And if you want to add in some variety to the trading, you can pick out different security to work with for that day.

You aren't restricted to just working with the stock market. Even though this is the most common place to work with trading, it isn't the only option available for you to choose from. You can someday trade with the Forex market, futures, options, cryptocurrencies, and the stock market.

Even though you will only stay in the market for a short amount of time with day trading, there are still a ton of strategies that you can choose to work with. These strategies allow you to work on different securities and market conditions. With day trading, you can do well with your trading regardless of what the market may be doing from one day to the other.

A lot of people like about day trading because it provides a huge potential for rewards. Many day traders are successful throughout the world, and they use their experience and their research to earn some big returns on every trade. Even beginners can see some great results as long as they are willing to learn and pay attention to the market. The highest rewards are some of the biggest reasons that so many people choose to get started with day trading.

Day trading provides you with the potential to earn an income from home each day, as long as you pick the right securities and the right strategies. It can take months or more to make any significant amount of money when it comes to long-term trades. The fact that you can make a good income from home each day is another reason some people love working with day trading.

With other forms of investing, you will hold onto your position overnight. There is always some risk of holding the position overnight because you never know when the price is going to drop and start lower the following day, and there is nothing you can do to prevent this when you are asleep. Day trading is going to get rid of this risk because you will exit the trade the night before, and never worries about your position going down in value. You need to know about the trading world and have a good idea about your risk tolerance, enough capital on hand, and realistic goals before you can get started with this as a viable career choice.

Remember that by reading this book, you will learn the option benefits you can enjoy when trading. This will help traders to know the market, resources, and how to work on different strategies. You don't have to apply everything you have learned at the same time. Take small steps every day and practice the strategies and tips to be a successful trader.

CHAPTER 1:

Options Basics

O ptions are a popular instrument that is used in the stock market. It is a great choice for beginners, as it will help them understand how the stock market works.

What are Options?

Options are security instruments that are easy to trade in. You do not have to go the lengths that you have to trade in stocks and can easily buy and sell options. Many types' of securities can be traded as options. The underlying security should be stated when you get into the deal so that you can do research on the same.

Types of Options?

Options can be of two main types, American options, and European options. You must understand these in order to deal with them.

American Options

American options refer to those that can be exchanged at any time even before the maturity or the expiry date of the options. Say for example you bought an option in May 2016 and it will mature in May 2017. If in December, you have the chance to sell the option and attain a profit from it then you can sell it freely. These form the most issued types of options.

European Options

These form the other types of options that are issued. European options unlike American options will not allow you to sell them any time. You must wait until they mature in order to do so. Even if it proves to be a good option to sell them in between, you will not be able to do so. This type is not popular anymore and is generally avoided by most traders.

Note that these are just names of the options and have no geographic relevance.

Concepts of Options

These are the different concepts of options.

Call option

The call option refers to the option to buy assets at an agreed price on or prior to a date. The date is agreed upon by the buyer and the seller. Generally, the seller has a say in it, as he will be looking to profit from the deal. During the same period, the buyer will hope for the price to rise so that he can get a good deal out of it.

Put option

The put option is the opposite of the call option. It refers to the option to sell certain assets at an agreed price on a chosen date. Here, the seller will hope for the price of the stock to drop so that the buyer will refuse to buy it and he will be left with the money paid as advance.

Trading Option Benefits

Easy to understand

The very first advantage of options is that the concept is easy to understand, and you can start investing in it at the earliest. You can go through the meaning and concepts again to understand it better. Many youngsters find it easy to start trading in options and prefer it to the other types of stock market investments.

Flexibility

Options, as you know, allow you to remain flexible. You can either buy the option or refuse to do so. You have enough time to think about the deal and can walk away from it if you think the deal is not a good idea. This flexibility is what appeals to many investors as they have the chance to prevent their hands from getting burnt. You can also extend the time in some cases if you wish to conduct some more research on the topic.

Low Risk

There is a sense of low risk that is attached to options. This is mainly because you have the chance to know if or not a particular deal will work for you. You have to take time out to study the deal and see if it is lucrative. Only then should you go ahead with it. The risk factor will always count when you are investing a lot of money into it and dealing with it on a daily basis.

High Returns

The options market has the capacity to leave you with big returns. You will be able to control a lot of money with just a small investment. There are stories of how people have made thousands of dollars with just a small investment. How much you invest in it is completely up to you. But even with a small initial investment you will be able to gain a lot from your options.

Many options

As you know, there are many underlying securities in the options markets. You can look for particular securities to invest in like say just stocks or just foreign investments. The choice is yours and you can choose something that will work best for you. But remember to diversify it and choose different options.

Trading Options Disadvantages

Risk

As you know, there are certain risks associated with trading in options. You have to exercise precaution and must not go all out at investing in a big way. The more precaution that you practice, the better it is for you. Try to understand everything that there is to about options first and only then should you invest with it. The risks involved will intensify because it is day trading. You have to remain alert and do as is right for you.

Low liquidity

You have to understand that options will have low liquidity. This means that they cannot be easily sold in the market. If you offer any of the underlying securities to the people in the market, then they might be a little apprehensive and find it tough to buy it from you. Even if it is a good security, they might still have their doubts about it. You have to sell it to them in such a way that they are convinced of its actual value. That can pose a challenge. The risk of illiquidity is what chases away many but if you understand how to sell options then you will not find it difficult.

Time lapse

One danger is that the options might take a little too much time to change in value. Maybe they will rise in value just a day after you refuse them owing to a fall in their prices. It is a little hard to predict the direction that these securities will take. You have to indulge in understanding the different prediction techniques if you wish to know whether or not the securities will do well. If you find it tough to do so, then you can take the help of a friend who is well versed in it. Don't make the mistake of getting into something that you don't know works or not. Even if you do, tell yourself that it is a learning curve.

Information

There can be some spurious information out there, which might throw you off and confuse you. If you are receiving any emails from sources that you cannot identify, then it is best that you do not entertain them at all. Turn a blind eye to it and continue with your trading. Many rookies make the mistake of believing what they see on the Internet, news or emails. They assume that they are reading what is good information and end up making investment mistakes. You surely don't want that happening to you, especially if you are just starting out.

Not for all securities

Remember that the options market is not open to all types of securities. There are only certain types like stocks, ETFs etc. So, if you are looking for something very specific then you might not find it in the options market. However, that is a good thing for some as the options reduce and you will not have to go through a lot of details to find the best one for yourself. Many times, people make the mistake of having a lot of options and then choose the wrong one. That will be successfully eliminated if you wish to trade with options.

Chapter Summary

Options are security instruments that are easy to trade in and popular instrument that is used in the stock market. It is a great choice for beginners, as it will help them understand how the stock market works. You do not have to go the lengths that you have to trade in stocks and can easily buy and sell options.

Options can be of two main types, American options, and European options. You must understand these in order to deal with them.

- American Options

- European Options

These are the different concepts of options.

- Call option

- Put option

Trading Option Benefits

- Easy to understand

- Flexibility

- Low Risk

- High Returns

Disadvantages

- Risk

16

- Low liquidity

- Time lapse

- Information

- Not for all securities

CHAPTER 2:

Day Trading Options Basics

T he options trading approach has more than one way. If you want to get in the thick of things, then being an options day trader is the right path for you.

What Options Day Traders Do

When a trader gets into trading, they are hopeful that everything will play out well and that they will start making a lot of profits in no time. To succeed in trading, a trader must know what trade all is about.

This means that they should fully be aware of the strategies in trading, risks involved, how to manage the risks, and, importantly, understand the psychology involved in the trade.

Trading involves you invest your money into the investment. It is essential for a beginner trader to fully understand the business before investing in large sums of money.

It is vital that as a trader, you understand how to stick to your methods no matter how tempting it gets. Sticking to your strategy shows that you trust your understanding of the market and cannot easily quit.

How to Get Started

The first thing to consider when getting started in day trading, is which market you want to use to trade. The important thing to recognize with day trading is that day traders routinely have strings of losses. Day trading isn't a hobby or a game. It's a serious business, and just like any serious business day, trading will require a serious commitment even before you get started.

Choose a broker

If you are already investing in stocks independently outside an employer or a mutual fund you may already have a broker that can also act as a broker for day trading purposes. Top brokers that retail investors can use include Ally Bank, TD Ameritrade, Trade Station, Interactive Brokers, ETrade, Charles Schwab, and many others.

Trading on the Stock Market

Experts advise that you need to have at least $25,000 in the capital that you can risk day trading to trade on the stock market. Making four trades in a week will qualify as being a day trader. If you plan to day trade four days per week, it's recommended that you have $30,000, to give yourself a bit of a buffer over the minimum. However, this value is quoted as assuming that you're going to be trading actual shares of stock. It is recommended that your maximum risk on trade be limited to 1% of your total capital.

It's important to know your risk and position risk. Position risk is the number of shares times the risk. Stocks with higher volatility will require more risk than stocks with lower volatility. A good way to get in on day trading on the stock market is by trading options. Buying an options contract only requires that you invest in the premium. Trading in options lets you leverage your money.

Futures Markets

You can day trade on futures markets with less capital. This can still let you get involved with stocks, however. For example, you can day trade the S&P 500 on the futures markets with a fraction of the capital required for day trading stocks. You can probably get started on this for between $1,000-$2,500. The daily range of futures can run from 10-40 points depending on volatility.

FOREX Markets

Forex markets are the lowest priced opportunity, with an entry level of capital of about $500. If you are interested in getting into day trading but lack capital, the FOREX markets can be considered to get started with day trading. Even though FOREX markets have smaller required minimum accounts, the same rules apply. Traders should not risk more than 1% of their capital on a single trade.

Planning for Success

Good traders make plans before every trade they enter to ensure that they are always making the best possible moves in the market. Great traders do not just make plans; they validate them against their notes, additional research, and other people's experiences to ensure that they have the best plans possible. Great traders know that getting involved in a trade deal can be stressful, and they want access to the best possible strategy before they go in so that they can execute their trades to the highest profits possible.

Remember that you never want to pivot or change a strategy once you are invested in a trade, so you need to make sure that you have the best strategy before going into your trade. This means you need to have your risk tolerance and maximum loss identified and validated as being a strong position, and you need to have your target profit made so that you know when to exit the market with your profits. You also need to outline how and when you will manage the trade, so you know exactly how often to check-in without being obsessive or unnecessarily stirring up stress inside yourself.

Your Goals

Understand your trading goals, as this will help you push on when the market doesn't seem to be working out well for you. The primary purpose of trading is to get money, but you should have a reason for why you need the money. Having the exact reason in your mind why you need the money will keep you more motivated to be a better trader every day. A clear objective will make you want to keep going even when you feel like giving up. You need to have stringent goals for yourself. Goals will assist you in working towards something that you need to accomplish. Visualize your goals so good and perform day trading towards them. Work hard and you will succeed in day trading.

Personal Development

Immediately when you start trading. You must identify your weaknesses. The earlier you learn about your shortcomings, the quicker you get to work on it before you are exposed to losing money. You will get to know if the weaknesses are something you could work on yourself or need help from other experienced traders. It is good to try working by yourself first since then, which means that you get to learn your weaknesses further. When this doesn't work out, then it is good to seek help from other traders.

Identifying your strength is essential as it will help you stop wasting time when you can follow your strengths to achieve an intended trade goal. Every trader is different; what one trader finds to be their weakness could be another trader's strength and vice versa. The trick is to identify what will do for you as a trader. The trader has to find out where they are going wrong and amend or replace the mistakes for better trading experiences.

Developing a Time Schedule

Have a schedule for your trading. Do not rush to trade immediately when the market opens. These are risky moments since the trades might be of the nights, and the market is not stable. You should know the best time to make your trade. Different market securities have a different time to trade. Do not be overexcited and do things anyhow. Have a timing plan for your trades.

Allow yourself time to adapt to the market, to know how trading works, and even understand the many risks you are likely to incur. Allowing yourself time to just adjust to the market without so much greed for the money will make you a great trader who will succeed in the long run.

Entry into the Options Trading Market

To survive in this game, you ought to know the entry plus that of exit prices. Day trading, like any other business, has worst-case scenarios. The entry price will help you understand when to get in while the exit point will help you know when to get out. With the prices, you will able to plan yourself on how to handle things in terms of market disasters with no worries.

The Qualities of an Effective Options Day Trader

Be Focused

Being focused will save you from lots of trouble. If you want to be successful, get yourself together and have strategies and plans on trading. Know when the right time is to make trades so as not to miss the golden time to do your trades.

Disciplined

Discipline is actually what it takes to be a successful day trader. Develop strict rules and don't trust emotions. Day traders can also use technical analysis.

Learn from Others

When you are trading, everyone else who is involved in trades is considered your competition. All of these people invest in the same market as you and behave in ways that you hope will result in you being able to take advantage of positions that will earn you more profits.

Consistent Research

One way that experienced traders manage to increase their skill level and become expert traders is through consistently engaging in informative research. Experienced traders never assume that they know everything, even if they have been successfully trading stocks for years. They know that patterns are always changing, the market is always evolving, and there is no way that they could ever know everything that there is to know about trading on the stock market.

Chapter Summary

A trader must know what trade all is about to succeed in trading. This means that they should fully be aware of the strategies in trading, risks involved, how to manage the risks, and, importantly, understand the psychology involved in the trade.

The first thing to consider when getting started in day trading, is which market you want to use to trade what broker to use.

- Trading on the Stock Market

- Futures Markets

- FOREX Markets

Planning for Success

Good traders make plans before every trade they enter to ensure that they are always making the best possible moves in the market.

Your Goals

Understand your trading goals, as this will help you push on when the market doesn't seem to be working out well for you. Goals will assist you in working towards something that you need to accomplish.

Personal Development

You must identify your weaknesses to learn your shortcomings and identifying your strength is essential as it will help you stop wasting time when you can follow your strengths to achieve an intended trade goal.

Developing a Time Schedule

Do not rush to trade immediately when the market opens. Allow yourself time to adapt to the market, to know how trading works, and even understand the many risks you are likely to incur.

Entry into the Options Trading Market

The entry price will help you understand when to get in while the exit point will help you know when to get out.

The Qualities of an Effective Options Day Trader

- Be Focused

- Disciplined

- Learn from Others

- Consistent Research

CHAPTER 3:

The Trading Market

U nderstanding the market trends gives the trader an upper hand as they know when to buy and when to sell their securities. A day trader should have sufficient market knowledge. Failing to study and understand the market will only make you fail in your day trading activity. It is imperative to understand the securities that are worth buying and those that you should stay away from.

Deciding What Market to Trade In

You have to consider several things when choosing your trading market. One of the most important factors is your financial position. If you can't afford to start trading $30,000, you'll have to skip the stock market and settle for the futures, cryptocurrency, or foreign exchange markets instead.

A trading system is required for a day trade. If you don't have the necessary equipment or software to day trade, you'll be very hard-pressed to succeed in day trading

Consider also the time zone. The United States isn't the only day trading market that can provide profit opportunities. There are other day trading markets around the world, i.e., different time zones. If you're a night owl, maybe financial markets from the other side of the pond may be more suited for you. If you're a day person, you shouldn't have a problem trading the United States markets.

Your personality and interests may also play essential roles in your ability to day trade successfully in specific markets.

When you have finally chosen your starting market, commit to sticking to it for the foreseeable future. Flipping back and forth between different markets isn't just stressful, but it can also impede your ability to master a particular market. Focus is the key.

How to Find the Best Options to Day Trade

If you'd like to start day trading in the United States' stock market, you'll need a minimum of $25,000 in your broker's account at all times. This means if your equity balance falls below this amount at any point, your day trading privileges may be suspended until you put in more money to meet the minimum amount. Your equity balance includes your cash balance and the current market value of the stocks you're holding.

Considering the highly volatile nature of day trades, you'll be better off starting with an equity balance higher than the minimum. Another popular day trading market is the futures market. As the name implies, this is the market to trade futures contracts, which are nothing more than formal agreements to buy or sell a specific number or amount of particular assets at a fixed price, regardless of what the price of such assets is in the future.

Day traders can make money day trading futures the same way they do with stocks, i.e., they buy futures contracts at a lower price and sell them at a higher price within the same trading day. Trading hours for futures markets aren't as fixed as those in the stock market. They depend on the kind of contracts involved. Pay close attention to the trading day's actual end for the type of contracts you're trading to avoid carrying an open position to the next one.

Once you start day trading, you can use several techniques and methods to execute trades. You can choose to trade based solely on your gut feeling. You can go to the other extreme of relying entirely on mathematical models that optimize trading success through elaborate automated trading systems. Regardless of the method, you can have limitless day-trading profit potential once you master day trading.

Technical Analysis

Indicators and charts are one of the essential components of technical analysis. It can represent different information and may appear in various forms. In the graphical analysis, the graphs deserve particular attention because they represent a given financial instrument's price dynamics and in a given period.

The analysis of the graphs is for particular shapes, also called graphic structures, configurations, figures. They are figures that emerge from the price movement, and that can signal its future trend. They are tracked by analysts joining points in the price graph of financial security or an indicator's performance. The purpose is to identify the most typical price patterns for forecasting.

Price Charts

Charts are used by traders to monitor price changes. These changes determine when to enter or exit a trading position. There are several charts used in day trading. Although these charts differ in functionality and layout, they typically offer the same information to day traders.

Line Charts

These are very popular in all kinds of stock trading. They do not give the opening price, just the closing price. You are expected to specify the chart's trading period to display the closing price for that period. The chart creates a line that connects closing prices for different periods using a line.

Most days, traders use this chart to establish how a security price has performed over different periods. However, you cannot rely on this chart as the only information provider when it comes to making some critical trading decisions. This is because the chart only gives you the closing price. This means that you may not establish other vital factors that have contributed to the current changes in the price.

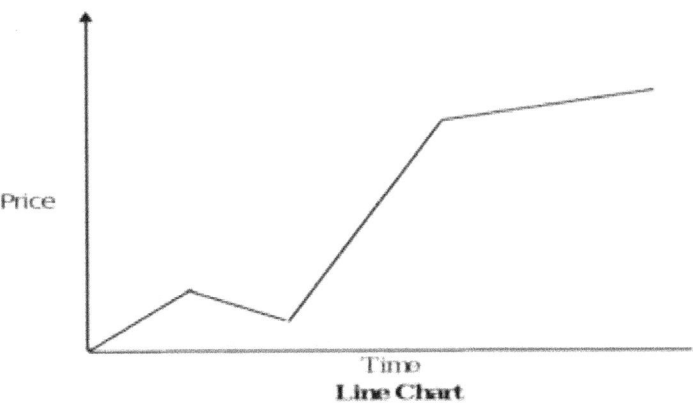

Line Chart

Open-Hight- Low-Close Bar Chart

These are lines used to indicate price ranges for a particular stock over time. Bar charts comprise vertical and horizontal lines. The horizontal lines often represent the opening and closing costs. The horizontal line is always black if the closing price is higher than the opening price. When the opening price is higher, the line becomes red.

Bar charts offer more information than line charts. They indicate opening prices, the highest and lowest prices as well as the closing prices. They are always easy to read and interpret. Each bar represents rice information. The vertical lines indicate the highest and lowest prices attained by a particular stock. The opening price of a stock is always shown using a small horizontal line on each vertical line's left. The closing price is a small horizontal line on the right.

When the vertical lines are long, it shows that there is a significant difference between the highest price attained by security and the lowest price. Therefore, large vertical lines indicate that the commodity is highly volatile, while small lines indicate slight price changes. When the closing price is far much higher than the opening price, it means that the buyers were more during the stated period.

Bar chart information is always differentiated using color codes. Therefore, you must understand what each color means, as this will help you know whether the price is going up or down.

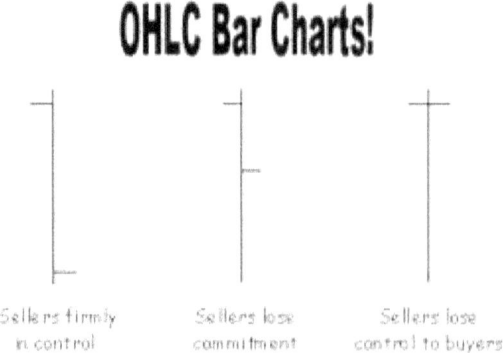

Candlesticks Chart

Candlestick charts are used on almost every trading platform. These charts carry a lot of information about the stock market and stock prices. They help you get information about the opening, closing, highest, and lowest stock prices.

The opening price is always indicated as the first bar on the left of the chart, and the closing price is on the chart's far-right. Besides these prices, the candlestick chart also contains the body and wick.

These are the features that differentiate the candlestick for other day trading charts.

One great advantage of candlestick charts entails using different visual aspects when indicating the closing, opening, highest, and lowest stock prices. These charts compute stock prices across different time frames. Each chart consists of three segments:

- The upper shadow

- The body

- The lower shadow

The body of the chart is often red or green. Each candlestick is an illustration of time. The data in the candlestick represents the number of trades completed within the specified time.

The high point represents the highest stock price while low stands for the lowest price of a stock.

The candlestick's body will be red when the closing price is lower than the opening price. If the closing price is higher, the body will be colored green.

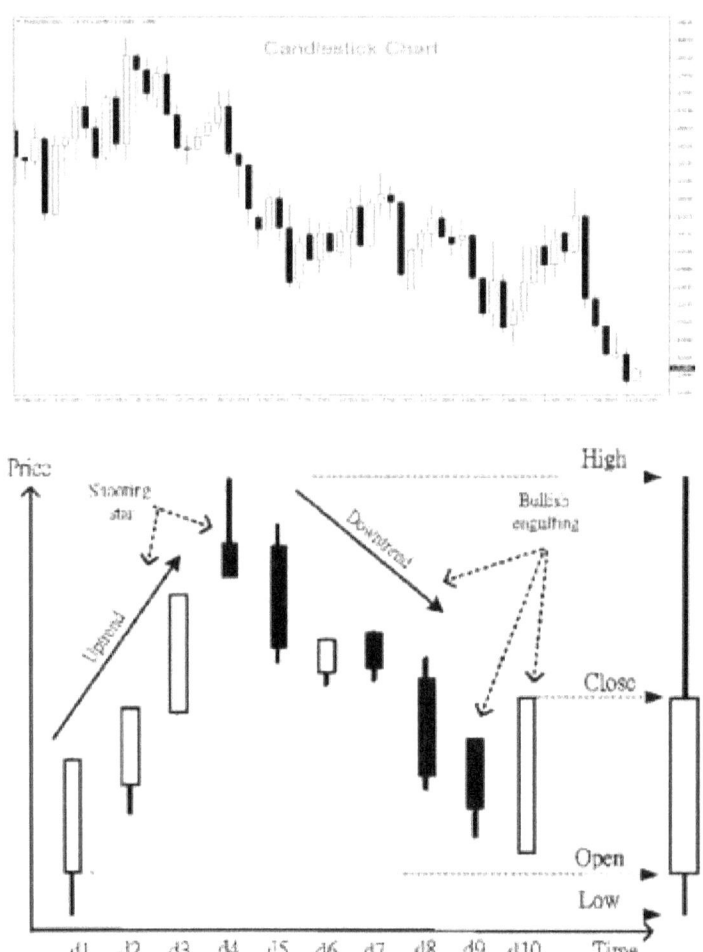

Factors That Affect Options Market

There are different options markets available. Options can be based on a variety of securities. Different traders have different needs and variations when it comes to options contracts. There are also various reasons why traders choose to deal in options rather than other financial instruments. There are a few factors that affect the options market.

Strike Price:

This is the price that you will sell or buy the underlying stock should you choose to exercise your options. Also called the exercise price.

Expiration Date:

The options contract is not indefinite and has an expiration date. The expiration date referred to the time when the contract entered into becomes void or expires.

Premium:

This term refers to the price you pay for the option. This price is charged per share, which means it will depend on the number of shares you sign up to. Premium has different components to it. These are the intrinsic value and time value of an option.

Intrinsic Value:

This is the value of an option and refers to the difference between the underlying stock's strike price and its current market price.

Time value:

The time value of a share refers to the amount of time available before an options contract expires. The time value decreases as the expiry date approaches. Time decay is the term used to express the approach of the expiration date. As this time decay progresses, the time value of an option decreases. This time is derived from the pricing model that was used to calculate it. Time is precious to investors hence the importance of time decay.

Chapter Summary

A day trader should have sufficient market knowledge to know when to buy and sell their securities. It is imperative to understand the securities that are worth buying and those that you should stay away from. You can use several techniques and methods to execute trades once you start day trading. You can have limitless day-trading profit potential once you master day trading regardless of the method.

Indicators and charts represent different information and may appear in various forms. The graphs deserve particular attention because they represent a given financial instrument's price dynamics and in a given period. Charts are used by traders to monitor price changes. These changes determine when to enter or exit a trading position. There are several charts used in day trading. Although these charts differ in functionality and layout, they typically offer the same information to day traders.

- Line Charts

- Open-Hight- Low-Close Bar Chart

- Candlesticks Chart

Factors that affect the options market are stock price, expiration date, premium, intrinsic value, and time value.

CHAPTER 4:

Options Day Trading Styles

N o matter what style or strategy an options day trader chooses to use, there are three essential components. These elements are:

Liquidity

This factor describes how quickly an option or other asset can be bought and sold without affecting the current market price. Liquid options are more desirable to an options day trader because they trade easier. It creates more resistance in the ease at which a trader can open or close their position. It expands the time needed to complete the transactions involved and can lead to a loss for the options day trader.

Volatility

This describes how sensitive the assets attached to the options are to price changes due to external factors. Some assets are more volatile than others. Stocks and cryptocurrencies are volatile assets. Volatility has a high impact on an options day trader's profit margin.

Volume

This describes the number of options being traded at a specific time interval. Volume indicates the associated assets price movement on the market because it is a gage of the asset's interest in the market. The higher the volume, the more desirable traders typically are in pursuing an option. Volume is one of the factors that make up open interest.

Breakout Options Day Trading

Breakout describes the process of entering the market when prices move out of their typical price range. For this style of trading to be successful, there needs to be an accompanying increase in volume. There is more than one type of breakout, but we will discuss one of the most popular support and resistance breakouts. The support and resistance method describe how the associated asset price stops decreasing (support) and the point at which the related asset price stops increasing (resistance). The day trader will enter a long position if the associated asset price breaks above resistance. On the other hand, the options day trader will enter a short position if the associated asset breaks below the supported price. As you can see, the trader's position depends on if the asset is supported or resisted at that new price level. As the asset transcends the normal price barrier, volatility typically increases. This usually results in the price of the associated asset moving in the direction of the breakout. The day trader will take on a bearish position if this price is said to be above the resistance level. A bullish approach is a typical maneuver if prices are set to close below the support. Exit strategies require a more sophisticated approach. The options day trader needs to consider past performance and use chart patterns to determine a price target to close their position. Once the goal has been reached, the day trader can exit the trade and enjoy its profit.

Momentum Options Day Trading

This options day trading style describes the process of options day trading relying on price volatility and the rate of change of volume. It is so-called because the main idea behind the strategy is that the force behind the associated asset's price movement is enough to sustain it in the same direction. This is because when an asset increases in price, it typically attracts investors, which drives the price even higher. Options day traders who use this style ride that momentum and profit from the expected price movement. This analysis gives the day trader an overall picture that includes momentum indicators like:

- The momentum indicator, which makes use of the most recent closing price of the associated asset to determine the strength of the price movement as a trend.

- The relative strength index (RSI), which is a comparison of profits and losses over a set period.

- Moving averages, which allows the day trader to see passed fluctuations to analyze the market trends.

- The stochastic oscillator, which compares the most recent closing prices of the associated asset over a specified time.

Momentum options day trading is highly effective and simple as long as it is done right. The day trader needs to keep abreast of the news and earnings reports to make informed decisions using this trading style.

Reversal Options Day Trading

This style relies on trading against the trend and the opposite of momentum options day trading. Also called trend trading or pull back trending, it is performed when an options day trader can identify pullbacks against the current price movement trends. It can be quite profitable when the trade goes according to plan. Because of the depth of market knowledge and trading experience needed to perform this style effectively, it is not recommended for beginners to practice.

Scalping Options Trading

This options day trading style refers to the process of buying and selling the same associated asset several times in the same day. This is profitable when there is extreme volatility on the market. The options day trader makes his profit by buying an options position at a lower price and sell it for a higher price. A trader can also sell options position at a higher price and buy it at a lower price depending on whether this is a call or a put option.

This style of options trading is extremely reliant on liquidity. Illiquid options should not be used with this style because the options day trader needs to be able to open and close these types of trades several times for one day. Trading liquid options allow the day trader to gain maximum profitability when entering and to exit trades.

Trading big with this particular style can lead to huge losses in the space of only a few hours. This is why this style is only recommended for disciplined options day traders who are content with seeking small, repeated profits even though it is a less risky method than the others.

It is the shortest form of options day trading because it does not even last the whole day – only a few hours. Day traders who practice this style are known as scalpers. Technical analysis is required to assess the best bets with the price movement of the associated assets.

Pivot Points Options Trading

This option day trading style is particularly useful in the forex market. It describes the act of pivoting or reserving after a support or resistance level has been reached at the market price. It is the same way with support and resistance breakouts.

The typical strategies with this particular options day trading style are:

- To buy the position if the support level is being approached, then placing a stop just below that level.

- To sell the position if the resistance level is being approached, then placing a stop just below that level.

To determine the point of a pivot, the day trader will analyze the highs and lows of the previous day's trading and the closing prices of the previous day. This is calculated with this formula:

(High + Low + Close) / 3 = Pivot Point

The pivot point can also calculate the support and resistance levels. The formulas for the first support and resistance levels are as follows:

(2 x Pivot Point) – High = First Support Level

(2 x Pivot Point) – Low = First Resistance Level

The second is calculated with the following formulas:

Pivot Point – (First Resistance Level – First Support Level) = Second Support Level

Pivot Point + (First Resistance Level – First Support Level) = Second Resistance Level

The options trading range that is most profitable lies when the pivot point is between the first support and resistance levels.

The options day trader is vulnerable to sudden price movements with his style of trading. This can result in serious losses if it is not managed. To limit losses with this strategy, the options day trader can implement stops to marginalize losses. The options day trader can also place two stops, such as placing a physical stop at the most capital that they can afford to part with and another where an exit strategy is implemented.

Chapter Summary

There are three essential components of Options day trading styles:

- Liquidity

- Volatility

- Volume

To take advantage of the options day trading, the trader needs to be very familiar with factors and use them:

Breakout Options Day Trading

Breakout describes the process of entering the market when prices move out of their typical price range.

Momentum Options Day Trading

This options day trading style describes the process of options day trading relying on price volatility and the rate of change of volume.

Reversal Options Day Trading

This style relies on trading against the trend and the opposite of momentum options day trading.

Scalping Options Trading

This options day trading style refers to the process of buying and selling the same associated asset several times in the same day.

This style of options trading is extremely reliant on liquidity

Pivot Points Options Trading

This option day trading style is particularly useful in the forex market. It describes the act of pivoting or reserving after a support or resistance level has been reached at the market price.

CHAPTER 5:

Options Trading Strategies

The following are option trading strategies that should get you trading in no time.

Covered Call Strategy

In this strategy, a trader buys a stock, and then they write a call option for that stock. The strategy generally works well on a stock that the investor is going long on. This means this is not a stock that you wish to speculate, but you would still like to receive some income while keeping it. And if you do sell it, you will sell it at a higher cost.

Here is the strategy in action. Say you own 300 shares of Lemonade Inc. that are currently going at $1.50. Then you write a call option at the strike rate of $1.70 per share, the premium you charge for this is 15¢ per share. If the stock price rises past $1.70 before expiration, let's say it is $1.90, the person you sold the call option will exercise their call option. You will be forced to sell 300 shares at the price of $1.70 per share, but since they will be paying a premium of 15¢ per share, you are selling your shares at $1.85 per share (strike price + premium) which is still high. The 5¢ that is left over is not the money that you lose. It is just money you missed out on. If Lemonade Inc.'s stock price does not rise sufficiently for the call option to be exercised, you will collect on the premium and still keep your shares. Regardless of what happens, you will leave with more money than you started with.

If you aim to keep the stock for a long time, this strategy is good to use, and you don't think the price will increase that much soon but still want to collect some money on that stock. This strategy is also referred to as a buy-write strategy. This even sounds better.

Iron Condor

An iron condor is a complex strategy. It is made to benefit from a small price movement, and it uses four call options. The first two are call options, one of them is long, and one of them is short. The second part is that the long and short options all share the same expiry date and the same underlying asset. You can put this strategy in place with a bearish or bullish. But in principle, the idea is to profit off a little movement.

The Calls

The first call in an iron condor strategy is a sold call closer to the money, while the second one is further out-of-the-money. Just like you would expect in credit call strategy.

The Puts

The first put in the iron condor strategy is a sold put option close to the money, and the second is a bought put option further out-of-the-money.

This allows the trader to cap his losses if he loses the difference between the bought and sold options, just like how it works in a credit call strategy. All options expire worthlessly, and the trader keeps all the premiums credited into his account. The best way to think of this strategy is to think of it as a credit call and credit put strategy. The trade received credit on the upside and the downside.

Straddle Strategy

The straddle is a very profitable strategy used in a market where high volatility is expected. So, you know that the price will move sharply, but you don't know which direction it will go. Regardless, you want to profit from that movement. To profit from an upswing, you buy a call option. To benefit from a fall, you buy a put option for the same asset for the same expiration date at the same strike price. You realize a profit when the money you make is more than the premium you have spent on both options. Now let's return to a Lemonade Inc. example to show this.

Let's say that Lemonade Inc. stock is trading at $100 per share. But you believe because of the pending company announcement, and the price will move sharply in either direction. You buy a call option for a $10 premium per share, and a put option for a $10 premium a share, both at a strike price of $100. You have $10,000 in your account. This will cost you a total of $2,000 in premiums. So, you are left with $8,000. The announcement is made before the expiry date of both options. Lemonade Inc. has experienced losses in the last quarter. Its stock fell by 30%, meaning it is now trading at $70 a share. In this situation, you can buy 100 shares at $70, costing you $7,000 and exercise your put option, selling them for $10,000. You have just made $3,000 on that transaction. You now have $11,000 in your account.

If the announcement made by Lemonade Inc. reports increases in sales and the stock rises by a record of 50%, you will be able to buy 100 shares at $100 and then sell them on the market for $150 each. Since you have $8,000 leftover, you can't afford to exercise your call option. But you use your margin account to borrow $2,000 and buy the shares at $10,000. You make $15,000 on the transaction. You pay your debt, plus interest, and it costs you $2,300. You are left with $12,700. You have made a profit of $4,700.

No matter the direction the stock moves, as long as it is beyond the premium you spent on the options, you made a profit. But if the market price moves only slightly, you will have lost $2,000, and you will be left with $8,000 in your account.

The Strangle

The strangle is similar to the straddle strategy, but instead of buying options that share the same strike price, asset, and expiry date, they buy two options that only share an expiry date and asset. So, the strike prices are different from each other. It is also a strategy often used in situations that are similar to that of a straddle. In both cases, the trader believes that the underlying stock price will move in some direction, but they do not know which. They might have a slight bias about where it might go, but they exercise the strangle to catch profits if they're mistaken. Just like the straddle, if the price does not move enough, the money will be lost on premiums. Time for that lemonade example.

The situation is much like before. Lemonade Inc. will announce, but the rumors around the report are positive, but investors are somewhat skeptical. The stock price is stable, but once the decision is made, the price might move sharply. Thinking the news might be positive, you buy a call option with a strike price at the current stock price. The stock is going at $100 per share. The premium costs you $10 a share. You think it is unlikely that the price will fall, but you want some money for yourself if it falls. You buy a put option at a $98 strike price for $8 a share. You have spent a total of $1,800 on the premiums. Already, this strategy is cheaper than straddle.

Once the stock price falls by 20%, you will collect a profit of $1,800, meaning you break even. If it rises sharply by 50%, you will rake in a profit of $5,000 from the transaction, that minus the premium paid is $3,200. If your bias was correct, you stand to make a few extra bucks that you would miss if using a straddle strategy. If your preference was wrong and the price falls sharply, you would still make money, but you will miss out on some of the action, although this doesn't translate to money lost. In both strategies, the price movement has to be sharp enough to overcome the premium spent. For instance, in a situation where Lemonade Inc.'s announcement doesn't sway the markets either way, and they remain relatively stable, you will have lost $1,800, which is $200 less than you would have in a straddle strategy.

Chapter Summary

Covered Call Strategy

- A trader buys a stock, and then they write a call option for that stock.

- The strategy generally works well on a stock that the investor is going long on.

The Straddle

- The straddle is a very profitable strategy used in a market where high volatility is expected.

- To profit from an upswing, you buy a call option.

- To benefit from a fall, you buy a put option for the same asset for the same expiration date at the same strike price.

- You realize a profit when the money you make is more than the premium you have spent on both options.

The Strangle

- The strangle is similar to the straddle strategy, but instead of buying options that share the same strike price, asset, and expiry date, they buy two options that only share an expiry date and asset.

- The price of the primary stock will move in some direction, but they do not know which.

- Just like the straddle, if the price does not move enough, the money will be lost on premiums.

Iron Condor

- It is made to benefit from a small price movement, and it uses four call options.

- The first two are call options, one of them is long, and one of them is short. The second part is that the long and short options all share the same expiry date and the same underlying asset.

- Like with the strangle, you can put this strategy in place with a particular bearish or bullish.

CHAPTER 6:

Credit Spreads

S preads can be classified in different ways. Credit spreads are distributed strategies that involve total receipts of premiums, while debit spreads include total payments of premiums. It entails promoting a high premium choice while buying a low premium choice in the same category or the same security, which leads to a credit on the trader's account.

The premium got from the written choice is higher than the premium settled for the long choice, leading to a high quality credited into the trader or maybe the investor's account whenever the position is opened. When traders or investors utilize a credit spread program, the maximum revenue they get will be the total premium. The credit spread leads to an income once the options' spreads narrow.

For instance, a trader tools a credit spread program by composing the 1st March call option with a strike price of $30 for $3 plus concurrently purchasing the 1st March call option with $40 for $1. Since the typical multiplier on an equity choice is a hundred, the web premium received is $200 because of the swap. Moreover, the trader is going to profit when the spread tactic narrows.

A bearish trader expects stock prices to reduce, therefore, and buys call choices (long call) in a particular hit cost and offers (short call) the same amount of call options inside the same category and the same expiration in a reduced hit selling price. In comparison, bullish traders expect stock prices to increase, and consequently, purchase call options in a particular hit cost and promote the same amount of call options inside the same category along with the same expiration in a greater hit selling price.

There are different types of credit spreads.

- Bear call spread, which is a beginner-friendly strategy. It employs a bearish outlook that relies on the price of the associated asset decreasing modestly. Profit is gained by finding the difference between the option premium and the commissions paid. Loss occurs when the asset price increases below the strike price.

- Bull put spread is a beginner-friendly strategy with a bearish outlook that relies on decreasing the associated asset price substantially. Profit is gained by finding the difference between the option premium and the commissions paid. Loss occurs when the asset price decreases below the strike price.

- Iron butterfly spread, which involves 4 transactions. The options trader is buying 1 out of the money call option, selling 1 at the money call option, buying 1 out of the money put option, and selling 1 at the money put option, all with the same expiration date and associated asset. This is a complex strategy that is not recommended for beginners.

- Short butter spread, which entails 3 transactions. The transactions are buying 1 out of the money call/put option, selling 1 out of the money call/put option, and buying 1 at the money call/put option with the same expiration date and associated asset. This is also a complex strategy that is not recommended for beginners.

Debit Spreads

A debit spread entails buying a high premium choice while offering a low premium choice in the same category and the same protection, which leads to debit from the trader's account.

Alternatively, a debit spread - usually utilized by beginners to option techniques - requires purchasing an option with a greater premium and concurrently selling an alternative with a reduced premium. The place that the premium settled for the lengthy choice of the spread is much more than the premium gotten from the written choice.

Compared with a credit spread, a debit spread leads to a high quality debited, or maybe given, out of the trader's or perhaps investor's account whenever the position is opened. Debit spreads are largely used to offset the expenses related to owning long features positions.

For instance, a trader buys, one could place a choice with a strike price of $20 for $5 and also instantly sells one could put an option with a strike price of $10for $1. Thus, he paid $4 and $400for the swap. In case the trade is from the money, the max loss of his is lowered to $400, instead of $500.

Different types of debit spreads

- Bear put spread requires 2 transactions and a bearish strategy, which are buying 1 at the money put option and the selling of 1 on the money put option. This is done because the trader is betting that the associated asset's price movement will go down. Profit is earned when the associated asset's price is the same as the strike price of the put option.

- Bull call spread, which is a bullish strategy that includes 2 transactions, which are the buying of 1 at the money call option and the selling of 1 out of the money call option. A trader implements this strategy when he or she thinks that the associated asset's price movement will go up modestly. Profit is gained when the associated asset's price is the same at the strike price of the short call option.

- Butterfly spread, which is a neutral strategy that involves 3 transactions whereby the trader buys 1 in the money call option, sells 2 at the money call option, and buys 1 on the money call option. Profit is gained when the price of the associated asset remained the same on the date of expiration.

- Reverse iron butterfly, which is a volatile strategy that involves 4 transactions. These transactions are selling 1 out of money put option, buying 1 at the money put option, buying 1 at the money call option, and selling 1 out of money call option. Profit is gained when the price of the associated asset falls.

Chapter Summary

A credit spread entails promoting a high premium choice while buying a low premium choice in the same category or the same security, which leads to a credit on the trader's account. There are different types of credit spreads:

- Bear call spread,

- Bull put spread

- Iron butterfly spread

- Short butter spread

A debit spread entails buying a high premium choice while offering a low premium choice in the same category and the same protection, which leads to debit from the trader's account.

There are different types of debit spreads, as well:

- Bear put spread

- Bull call spread

- Butterfly spread

- Reverse iron butterfly

CHAPTER 7:

Rolling Out Options

A rollout is a strategy used to extend the lifetime of an option that hasn't quite worked out. This is going to be a strategy used by options sellers. A rollout might be something you would consider doing when you've sold a naked call, and the share price is closing in on your strike price, creating a risk that the option will be exercised. By doing a rollout, you can keep the trade going longer, and possibly make some changes to give the trade better odds of being profitable. Typically, you will choose to do a rollout when it is close to the expiration date.

A rollout strategy works in the following way. You will close your current option contract by buying it back, and simultaneously open a new contract of the same type, with changes. One way to change is by altering the strike price. Another more common method is to move up the expiration date. A common practice is to open the new contract with an expiration date that is further out in the future. For example, you could close a naked put option that is expiring in two days by buying it back and opening a new contract by selling a new naked put option. You would use the same stock and the same strike price but with an expiration date three weeks into the future. This is a standard strategy where we say that the option contract was rolled out.

You can also follow the same strategy choosing either a higher strike price or a lower strike price. For example, if we have an Apple naked put with a strike price of $205, we could roll up the option by closing this position and selling a new naked put on Apple with a strike price of $206. Alternatively, you could choose a lower strike price. Using the same example, instead of going with a $206 strike price, we could go with a $203 strike price. Maybe, in that case, the Apple share prices are dropping, and it got a little too close for comfort. When you select a lower strike price, they say that you have rolled down the trade.

It's also possible to roll out and roll up or down. You can close your current contract and open a new one that has a further expiration date, but you also change the strike price.

Types of Options Where Rolling Strategies Are Used

You can use a rollout, roll up, or roll down strategy on any option, including options that you buy to open (long calls and puts). However, the vast majority of options contracts that are rolled are short (buy to open) options. You can use rolling techniques on important strategies such as put credit spreads, strangles, or iron condors. The main reason that options traders roll an option contract is that they are in the money, and there is an assignment risk. By rolling it out, you can keep the trade going but avoid assignment. Sometimes just moving the expiration date is good enough to accomplish this. An option can be assigned at any time, but it has to reach expiration to be assigned in most cases. By using a rollout, the trader can avoid this situation. Of course, rolling up or rolling down can also help avoid assignment, since changing the

strike price might allow you to move from an in the money situation to an out of the money situation.

Other reasons are sometimes used to justify rolling an option. For example, when you are selling for income, you can roll the trade to keep generating more money. Changing market conditions might also be a reason to roll a trade.

When rolling a spread, strangle, or iron condor, many possibilities exist for altering the trade. Suppose you have a put credit spread with strikes of $207 and $204. We could change one or both of the strike prices, and we could also change the expiration date. Maybe we want to tighten or widen the spread, roll out and roll down the lower strike price, and have a new spread with strike prices of $207 and $202, for example. It's important to note that a rollout is one trade, and not two. You are simultaneously closing one option (possibly with multiple legs) and opening a new contract.

Chapter Summary

A rollout is a strategy used to extend the lifetime of an option that hasn't quite worked out. It is considered when you've sold a naked call, and the share price is closing in on your strike price, creating a risk that the option will be exercised.

- You will choose to do a rollout when it is close to the expiration date.

- You can also follow the same strategy choosing either a higher strike price or a lower strike price.

- It is possible to roll out and roll up or down.

- You can close your current contract and open a new one with a further expiration date, but you also change the strike price.

Types of Options Where Rolling Strategies Are Used

You can use a rollout, roll up, or roll down strategy on any option, including options that you buy to open (long calls and puts).

- The majority of options contracts that are rolled are short (buy to open) options. By using a rollout, the trader can avoid this situation.

- Rolling up or rolling down can also help avoid assignment since changing the strike price might allow you to move from an in the money situation to an out of the money situation.

- It's important to note that a rollout is one trade, and not two. You are simultaneously closing one option (possibly with multiple legs) and opening a new contract in its place.

CHAPTER 8:

Principles to Success in Options Day Trading

When a trader gets into trading, they are hopeful that everything will play out well and that they will start making a lot of profits in no time. To succeed in trading, a trader must know what trade is all about. This means that they should fully be aware of the strategies in trading, risks involved, how to manage the risks, and, importantly, understand the psychology involved in the trade.

Principle #1 Ensure Good Money Management

Money is the tool that keeps the engine of the financial industry performing in good working order. It is important to learn how you manage your money in a way that works for you instead of against you as an options day trader. It is an intricate part of managing your risk and increasing your profit.

Money management is the process whereby monies are allocated for spending, budgeting, saving, investing, and other processes. Money management is a term that any person with a career in the financial industry, and particularly in the options trading industry, is intimately familiar with because this allocation of funds is the difference between a winning options trader and a struggling options trader.

Money Management Tips for Options Traders

- Define money goals for the short term and the long term to envision what you would like to save, invest, etc. Ensure that these are recorded and easily accessed. Your trading plan will help you define your money goals.

- Develop an accounting system. There are wide ranges of software that can help with this. It does not matter which one you use as long as you can establish records and easily track your money flow.

- Use the position sizing to manage your money and determine how much money will be allocated to entering an options position. To do this effectively, allocated a smart percentage of your investment funds toward individual options.

- Never invest money you cannot afford to lose. Do not let emotion override this principle and cloud your judgment.

- Spread your risks by diversifying your portfolio. You diversify your portfolio by spreading your wealth by investing in different areas, add to your investments regularly, being aware of commissions at all times, and knowing when to close a position.

- Develop the day trading styles and strategies that earn you a steady rate of return. Even if you use scalping where the returns are comparatively small, that steady flow of profit can add up big over time.

Principle #2 Risk and Reward Should Be Balanced

To ensure that losses are kept to a minimum and that returns are as great as they can be, options day traders should use the risk/reward ratio to determine each and make adjustments as necessary. The risk/reward ratio is an assessment used to show the profit potential for potential losses. This requires knowing the potential risks and profits associated with an options trade. Potential risks are managed by using a stop-loss order. A stop-loss order is a command that allows you to exit a position in an options trade once a certain price threshold has been reached.

Profit is targeted using an established plan. The potential profit is calculated by finding the difference between the entry price and the target profit.

Another way to manage risks and rewards is by diversifying your portfolio. Always spread your money across different assets, financial sectors, and geographies. Ensure that these different facets of your portfolio are not closely related to each other so that if one goes down, others will not fall. Be smart about protecting and building your wealth.

Principle #3 Develop A Consistent Monthly Options Trading System

The aim of doing options trading is to have an overall winning options trading month. That will not happen if you trade options here and there. You cannot expect to see a huge profit at the end of the month if you only performed 2 or 3 transactions.

You need to have a high options trading frequency to up the chances of coming out winning every month. Develop a system where you perform options trades at least 5 days a week.

To have consistently good months, you need to develop strong daily systems that keep your overall monthly average high. Therefore, creating a daily options trading schedule is key. Here is an example of an efficient options day trading schedule:

- Perform market analysis. This needs to be done before the markets open in the morning. That means that the options day trader needs to get an early start on the day. This entails checking the news to scan for any major events that might affect the markets that day, checking the economic calendar, and assessing other day traders' actions to assess volume and competition.

- Manage your portfolio. The way that an options day trader does this is dependent on the strategies that he or she implements.

Overall, it is about assessing positions that you already have or are contemplating for efficient management of entry and exits. It also allows for good money management.

- Enter new positions. After assessing the market and fine-tuning your portfolio, the next step is to enter new trades that day. Research and efficient decision-making go into this step. The options trader who has already determined how the market was doing and forecasted performance that day would have noticed relevant patterns.

- Incorporate learning during the day. Continual learning is something that an option trader needs to pursue, but this does not always have to be formal classes or courses. You can up your knowledge of options and day trading.

Principle #4 Choose the Right Broker for Your Level of Option Expertise

You have to choose a broker that has an established and long-standing reputation for trading options. You also want to deal with a brokerage firm with great customer service, which can help lay the groundwork for negotiating reduced commissions and allow for flexibility.

There are four essential components that you need to consider when choosing a broker:

- The requirements for opening a cash and margin account.

- The unique services and features that the broker offers.

- The commission fees and other fees charged by the broker.

- The reputation and level of options expertise of the broker.

Broker Cash and Margin Accounts

Every options trader needs to open a cash account and margin account to be able to perform transactions. They are simply tools of the trade. A cash account allows an options day trader to perform transactions via being loaded with cash. Margin accounts facilitate transactions by allowing that to borrow money against the value of security in his or her account. Both of these types of accounts require that a minimum amount be deposited. This can be as few as a few thousand dollars to tens of thousands of dollars, depending on the broker of choice. You need to be aware of the requirements when deliberating, which brokerage firm is right for you.

Broker Services and Features

There are different types of services and features available from different brokerage firms. For example, if an options trader wants to have an individual broker assigned to him or her to handle his or her account personally, he or she will have to look for a full-service broker. In this instance, there minimum account requirements that need to be met. Also, commission fees and other fees are generally higher with these types of brokerage firms. While the fees are higher, this might be better for a beginner trader to have that full service dedicated to their needs and the learning curve.

The advantage to discount brokerage firms is that they tend to have lower commissions and fees. Most internet brokerage firms are discount brokers.

Other features that you need to consider when choosing a brokerage firm include:

- Whether or not the broker streams real-time quotes.

- The speed of execution for claims.

- The availability of bank wire services.

- The availability of monthly statements.

- How confirmations are done, whether written or electronic.

Commissions and Other Fees

Commission fees are paid when an options trader enters and exits positions. Every brokerage firm has its commission fees set up. These are typically developed around the level of account activity and account size of the options trader.

Many brokerage firms charge penalty fees for withdrawing funds and not maintaining minimum account balances—obviously, the existence of fees such as these cuts on any options trader's profit margin. The payment of fees needs to be kept to a minimum to gain maximum income, and as such, an options trader needs to be aware of all fees that exist and how they are applied when operating with a brokerage firm.

Chapter Summary

To succeed in trading, a trader must know what trade all is about.

Principle #1 Ensure

Money management is the process whereby monies are allocated for spending, budgeting, saving, investing, and other processes.

Principle #2 Risk and Reward Should Be Balanced

The risk/reward ratio is an assessment used to show the profit potential for potential losses.

Principle #3 Develop A Consistent Monthly Options Trading System

You need to have a high options trading frequency to up the chances of coming out winning every month. Develop a system where you perform options trades at least 5 days a week.

Principle #4 Choose the Right Broker for Your Level of Option Expertise

Options trading is a complex service, and your brokerage firm needs to provide support when handling difficult transactions.

CHAPTER 9:

Options Day Trading Rules for Success

T o develop into the options day trader you want to be, being disciplined is necessary. There are options day trading rules that can help you develop that necessary discipline.

Knowing common mistakes helps you avoid many of these mistakes and takes away much of the guesswork. Having rules to abide by helps you avoid these mistakes as well.

Rule #1 Be mentally, physically and emotionally prepared every day

This is a mentally, physically, and emotionally tasking career, and you need to be able to meet the demands of this career. That means keeping your body, mind, and heart in good health at all times. Ensure that you schedule a time for self-care every day. That can be as simple as taking the time to read for recreation to having elaborate self-care routine carved out in the evenings.

Not keeping your mind, heart, and head in optimum health means that they are more likely to fail you. Signs that you need to buckle up and care for yourself more diligently include being constantly tired, being short-tempered, feeling preoccupied, and being easily distracted.

To ensure you perform your best every day, here a few tasks that you need to perform:

- Get the recommended amount of sleep daily. This is between 7 and 9 hours for an adult.

- Practice a balanced diet. The brain and body need adequate nutrition to work their best. Include fruits, complex carbs, and veggies in this diet and reduce the consumption of processed foods.

- Eat breakfast lunch and dinner every day. Fuel your mind and body with the main meals. Eating a healthy breakfast is especially important because it helps set the tone for the rest of the day.

- Exercise regularly. Being inactive increases your risk of developing chronic diseases like heart disease, certain cancers, and terrible health consequences. Exercise reduces those risks and allows your brain to function better, which is a huge advantage for an options day trader.

Rule #2 Know your limits

You may be tempted to trade as much as possible to develop a winning monthly average, but that strategy will have the opposite effect and land you with a losing average. Remember that every options trader needs careful consideration before that contract is set up. Never overtrade and tie up your investment fund.

Rule #3 Start a small to grow a big portfolio

Start Small to Grow a Big Portfolio

Remember that you are still learning options trading and developing an understanding of the financial market. Do not jump the gun even if you are eager. After you have practiced paper trading, start with smaller options positions, and steadily grow your standing as you get a lay of the options day trading land. This strategy allows you to keep your losses to a minimum and develop a systematic way of entering positions.

Rule#4 Have a realistic expectation

It is sad to say that many people who enter the options trading industry are doing so to make quick money. Options trading is not a get-rich-quick scheme. It is a distinguished career that has made many people rich, but that is only because these people have put in the time, effort, study, and dedication to learning the craft and mastering it. Mastery does not happen overnight, and beginner options day traders need to be prepared for that learning curve and have the courage to stick with day trading options even when it becomes tough.

Losses are also part of the game. No trading style or strategy will guarantee gains all the time. The best options traders have a winning percentage of about 80% and a losing average of approximately 20%. That is why an options day trader needs to be a good money manager and a good risk manager. Be prepared for eventual losses and be prepared to minimize those losses.

Rule#5 Do your homework daily

You need to get knowledge so that you have the basis for making decisions. When you know all there is to know about options, you know what to buy and when to sell, and learn which ones to watch. You are then more comfortable making the right decisions. Always evaluate your choices and see what you have gained or lost so far for taking some steps. Understanding the mistakes, you made guides you to make better decisions in the future.

Rule#6 Analyze your daily performance

To determine if the options day trading style and strategies that you have adopted are working for you, you need to track your performance. At the most basic, this needs to be done because you are trading options daily. It allows you to notice patterns in your profit and loss. This can lead to you determining the why and how of these gains and losses. These determinations lead to fine-tuning your daily processes for maximum returns.

Rule#7- Do not be greedy

This refers to a selfish desire to get more money than you need from a trade. When the desire to get more than you can usually make takes over your decision-making process, you are looking at failure.

Greed is seen to be more detrimental than fear. It places you in a situation where you spend your capital faster than you return it. It pushes you to act when you should not be acting at all.

When you are greedy, you end up acting irrationally. Irrational trading behavior can be overtrading, overleveraging, holding onto trades for too long, or chasing different markets. The more greed you have, the more foolish you act. If you reach a point at which greed takes over from common sense, you are overdoing it.

Rule#8 Pay attention to volatility

Volatility speaks to how likely a price change will occur over a specific amount of time on the financial market. Volatility can work for an options day trader or against the options day trader. It all depends on what the options day trader is trying to accomplish and his or her current position.

Many external factors affect volatility, and such factors include the economic climate, global events, and news reports. Strangles and straddles strategies are great for use in volatile markets.

There are different types of volatility, and they include:

- Price volatility describes how the price of an asset increases or decreases based on the supply and demand of that asset.

- Historical volatility, which is a measure of how an asset has performed over the last 12 months.

- Implied volatility, which is a measure of how an asset will perform in the future.

Rule9# Use the Greeks

Option traders use the Greeks to measure risk in their option positions and their combined positions or portfolios. Greeks are extremely important, and it should be the goal of anyone wanting to trade or invest in options to gain an intuitive understanding. An intuitive understanding of the Greeks will provide you with an understanding of the risk in your option position(s) and greatly contribute to your success as an options trader.

Delta

The Delta represents the amount the value of the option should change with a $1 move (up or down) in the Underlying stock price. Delta means change.

Vega

Vega measures the impact of a 1.00% change in volatility on the theoretical value of an option. It is important to monitor Vega to properly understand the risk in both your long and short positions.

Theta

Theta measures the general daily decay of the option premium, assuming no changes in the stock price and volatility. The life of an option is finite with a defined expiration and, therefore, every day, it decays in value—Theta measures this decay.

Gamma

Gamma simply represents the Delta's change for a given change in the underlying stock—it is the "Delta of the Delta."

Gamma shows the potential for your option position to "move" in terms of value. Note that Gamma can be either positive or negative.

Positive Gamma is generally good for your position, and negative Gamma is generally bad for your position.

Rho

Rho is a measure of the options pricing's sensitivity to a change in the risk-free interest rate. Since interest rates don't change by that much or that often these days, Rho isn't paid much attention to.

Rule#10 Be flexible

Many options day traders find it difficult to try trading styles and strategies they are unfamiliar with. While the saying, "Do not fix it if it is not broken," is quite true, you will never become more effective and efficient in this career if you do not step out of your comfort zone at least once in a while. Stick with want work but allow room for the consideration that there may be better alternatives.

Chapter Summary

Being disciplined is necessary to develop into the options day trader you want to be. There are options day trading rules that can help you develop that necessary discipline.

Rule #1 Be mentally, physically and emotionally prepared every day

Rule #2 Know your limits

Rule #3 Start a small to grow a big portfolio

Rule#4 Have a realistic expectation

Rule#5 Do your homework daily

Rule#6 Analyze your daily performance

Rule#7- Do not be greedy

Rule#8 Pay attention to volatility

There are different types of volatility, and they include:

- Price volatility

- Historical volatility

- Implied volatility

Rule9# Use the Greeks

- Delta

- Vega

- Theta

- Gamma

- Rho

Rule#10 Be flexible

CHAPTER 10:

Common Mistakes to Avoid

T here is a lot to learn in options trading as a beginner. It is a world far more complex than trading other securities. A lot is depending on the assumption of the market and the performance of the market in reality. Even the best and most informed guess can and would go wrong. Even the best of the world's traders can't say that they've never been wrong with their assumptions. They don't expect the market to move according to them but change their course of action according to the market.

Starting Without a Plan

Choosing the right option is one of the biggest decisions you will have to make in the trade. Most people don't devote any time to this. If you are planning to do any such thing, then you better donate your capital to charity. It will be put to better work, and you are anyway not going to get anything out of it.

Spend a lot of time in choosing the right stock. Look at the historical movement in the stock. Its performance over short-term and long-term, the volatility in the stock, and the kind of volume it enjoys. All these factors are very important and will play a key role in determining the stock's performance in the market.

Remember that the options contract that you are buying at a specific strike price will have to achieve it within a specific time frame for you to achieve any profit. This is a prediction that will take a lot of hard work.

Assumption of Knowledge

Some people have an assumption that they understand things deeply than others without having any data to prove that. Such people should stay away from options trade. This is a field where knowledge can make a lot of difference, and ignorance can make you lose everything you have.

Options trading is not easy. It is lucrative. It is rewarding. It is anything but easy. The strategies that may not be assuring great returns but will have the lowest risk are the most complex ones. The strategies that offer the highest reward with the lowest capital are the riskiest because they highly expose you to the market risks. You must have a complete understanding of these concepts when you enter the market.

You must understand that all the traders know about the long call and long put options, yet they invest in complex strategies in which they have to invest a lot to get limited returns. They do this because they understand the risk. You will also have to completely understand the risks and trade with strategies that can help you remain secure in the market. You will have to remain consistent if you want to survive in the market for the long-term.

Hesitation to Adopt New Strategies

One thing should be clear in your mind that no strategy is perfect and foolproof. There will be times when a strategy works, and in other scenarios, it won't. You can't remain stuck with one strategy all the time. When you change the trades, the scenarios change with it. You must have the vision to identify the new challenges in front of you and modify your strategy accordingly.

Remember that no strategy is perfect, and you must always remain open to change. No trader should stick to any one strategy for all kinds of situations.

Not Forming an Exit Strategy

Having a good and timely exit plan is a trademark of a good trader. If you see a trade performing poorly and if you still sit with your fingers crossed, hoping against hope for the things to improve, then you can be a great optimist, but you will certainly be a poor or, in fact, a very poor trader.

A good trader will have the foresight to see the implied risk in the trade and the time when the risk increases too much. In case you still have the time to cover some of the losses by squaring off your position, there should be no shame in doing that.

This is an undeniable fact that markets can be very volatile, and the tables might turn at the last moment. In that case, this step can prove to be unwise.

Think of an exit strategy for every trade. Select a point after which staying in that trade would be unreasonable as the chances of recovery of that trade would be extremely low. You must tick that box in your mind and get out of that trade. Later on, even if that trade performs, there is nothing that should worry you as this is not an event that is going to repeat itself very often, but if you don't, you'll see bigger losses very often.

Unreasonable Risk-Appetite

This is another problem with newcomers in options trading. They believe that they have come with the intention of double or nothing. No matter how deep your pockets run but they are bound to get empty very soon if you maintain high risk-appetite.

You must have a reasonable understanding of risk, and you must acknowledge it. You can't keep writing off risks like you are buying lottery tickets and waiting for that once in a lifetime jackpot.

Before you enter a trade, you must evaluate the amount of risk you are ready to take in that strategy. Several strategies limit your risk to a great extent. There is no doubt that they also limit your profit. If you are really into trading, you shouldn't have any problem with a greater number of low paying trades then a fewer number of trades with somewhat higher profit margins and a higher number of loss-making trades.

Not Ready to Take a Beating

As a trader, you can't be adamant. This is a tendency that generally gamblers have. They become more aggressive with every losing trade and keep increasing the bets with the hope that they'll make up for all they've lost in a single trade they win. A trader must think more rationally. Initially, make it a rule to invest a fixed amount in a trade. Even if a trade has gone against you, don't invest more in another trade. Stick with your plan and invest the amount up to which you can take the risk easily. Trading is a very different kind of world. Here, only those people can survive who remain consistent. Even these people take risks, but their risks are always contained. They don't go on a betting spree. They know when to accept defeat and strategize.

Time Frames are Important

This is last but not the least. Time is one of the most important factors in the options trade, as it is decaying fast. All the options contracts come with a predefined expiry. The longer you wait, the faster the degradation would take place in the trade and hence it would be a wise step to keep the time always in sight.

Many traders believe that a trade that's already in profit must be kept till the very end. As a new trader, if the trade is highly volatile, your focus should remain on booking your profit at a reasonable price well with the time limits of the trade. You must understand that near the expiry, the markets can get highly volatile. A trade that might have been looking very lucrative can take a nosedive without much warning, and if you don't have a cover strategy, your loss can be very high.

Always try to focus on a higher number of successful trades. As you gain more experience, your understanding of the market would also improve, and you will be more equipped to take the trades to their deep end. Until you reach that stage, remember that you can only trade as long as you maintain your investment capital and keep building it up.

Chapter Summary

An option trading is more complex than trading other securities. It is a derivative. A lot is depending on the assumption of the market and the performance of the market in reality.

- Starting Without a Plan

- Assumption of Knowledge

- Hesitation to Adopt New Strategies

- Not Forming an Exit Strategy

- Unreasonable Risk-Appetite

- Not Ready to Take a Beating

- Time Frames are Important

CHAPTER 11:

The Platforms and Tools

For you to carry out day trading successfully, there are several tools that you need. Some of these tools are freely available, while others must be purchased. Modern trading is not like the traditional version. This means that you need to get online to access day trading opportunities.

Brokerage

You need the services of a brokerage firm. The work of the firm is to conduct your trades. Some brokers are experienced in day trading than others. You must ensure that you get the right day trading broker who can help you make more profit from your transactions.

Since day trading entails several trades per day, you need a broker that offers lower commission rates.

You also need one that provides the best software for your transactions.

If you prefer using specific trading software for your deals, look for a broker that allows you to use it.

Real-time Market Information

Market news and data are essential when it comes to day trading. They provide you with the latest updates on current and anticipated price changes on the market. This information allows you to customize your strategies accordingly. Professional day traders always spend a lot of money seeking this kind of information on news platforms, online forums, or other reliable channels.

Financial data is often generated from price movements of specific stocks and commodities. Most brokers have this information. However, you will need to specify the kind of data you need for your trades. The type of data to get depends on the type of stocks you wish to trade.

Monitors

Most computers have a capability that enables them to connect to more than one monitor. Due to the nature of the day trading business, you need to track market trends, study indicators, follow financial news items, and monitor price-performance simultaneously.

Classes

Although you can engage in day trading without attending any school, you must train some of the strategies you need to succeed in the business. For instance, you may decide to enroll for an online course to acquire the necessary knowledge in the business. You may have all the essential tools in your possession, but if you do not have the right experience, all your efforts may go to waste.

Charting Software

Each of the above charts is created and viewed using specific software. This can be found in a brokerage firm, although you may also purchase this online depending on the type you want to use.

The software helps you identify the right opportunities by indicating when and how you should start and close positions. They always display the necessary patterns required to estimate future changes in stock prices. Using stock patterns, you can also establish continuations as well as reversals in the stock prices.

Chart software is available in many forms. You may find those that are in the form of mobile apps or others that are web-based. Getting the right software enables you to generate correct charts. This explains why you also need to incorporate technical analysis into your trades.

Most day trading chart tools are available free of charge. Some have a forum where you can learn from experienced traders as you use them. They also come with demo accounts that enable you to master day trading techniques before investing in your business capital.

How to Choose Day Trading Charts

Before selecting any charts for your day trading engagements, you must consider several factors. These include:

Responsiveness - This refers to how quickly the chart can display information about the changing market features. This is the first and most important factor you should always check out for. Any delay in the way a chart displays data means that you will not receive vital information in real-time. You may end up acting on old information to make your decisions, which can lead to significant losses on your part.

Most charts may freeze or crash when your computer runs out of memory. This explains why you need a fast processing machine for your day trading business. You want to ensure that the whole process remains as efficient as possible. When testing a chart for responsiveness, wait for a time when the stock market is busy.

For instance, you may try using the chart during a critical financial announcement or news session. If the chart freezes at this point, you will understand that it is not the best one.

Cost – every trader wants to invest in tools that cost less to acquire and maintain. Years back, trading charts used to cost a fortune. This limited the number of traders that could engage in day trading. For instance, traders could buy market data from stock exchanges, and this would also cost a lot of money. Nowadays, all information required for any kind of trading is cheaply available. This means that charts should also not cost as much. There are several alternatives available on the market today for you to select from. As you do this, always have the price in mind.

Stability – a good chart is one that remains online and up to date all the time. For you to succeed as a day trader, you must remain on the market most of the time. If your chart keeps disconnecting from the stock market or fails to display market information on time, then it will make you incur more losses.

You must, therefore, ensure that you remain connected to the market continuously. If you experience instability due to the chart software you are using, feel free to change it. If the instability is resulting from a poor Internet connection, you may need to replace it too.

Type of Indicators – if you have ever engaged in day trading before you understand the importance of technical indicators. Having the right indicators plays a vital role in ensuring you predict the right price movements. Indicators help you to save a lot of capital. They prevent you from making important investments and financial mistakes that may lead to losing your capital.

You may create your indicators, or you may get charting software that has in-built indicators. If you decide to use your indicators, you must ensure that the charting tools you purchase can be used together with these indicators. If not, you might need to stick to those indicators supplied together with your charting software.

Compatibility with your computer – before settling for any charts, check whether it will work well with your current computer resources. This will determine whether you will continue to use your old machine, or if you will have to purchase a new one. Some charts require a lot of RAM space.

If your computer does not have this capability, you will end up adding more RAM. This translates to more yet unnecessary costs. When you are looking around for a chart, ensure that you check how much resources the charts will need.

Most chart packages indicate the minimum requirements you need for the charts to work well. If this is not clearly stated, make sure you ask your provider about it so that you do not make a blind purchase.

User-friendly - a good chart should be easy to use, read, and interpret. A complicated chart will only make your trading days difficult. Get a chart that simplifies the work of interpreting data. Take your time and research on the available options then choose the best in terms of simplicity and layout.

You may consider getting recommendations from other traders, although this does not necessarily mean that the said chart will work for you. Having a complicated chart can make you lose your confidence. You must, therefore, avoid it if you want to have a smooth trading experience

End-user support – once in a while, your chart software may experience a problem that needs technical assistance. As you continue using the software, questions may arise that need the attention of an expert. If the provider is not available to assist or respond to your questions, you may get stuck using the package.

Before making a purchase, ensure that you find the kind of technical support you will receive and how this will be done.

In case you need a highly responsive system, you may need to avoid those platforms that use the support ticket criteria. Companies that use this criterion to solve customer problems always take a long time to respond to even the most critical issues.

Charts play an essential role, and you can use timed and ticked charts for successful day trading. Always remember that different tools are designed for different kinds of trades. You must understand the tools you need as a day trader, so you do not struggle in the market.

Chapter Summary

For you to carry out day trading successfully, there are several tools that you need.

Brokerage

You need the services of a brokerage firm. The work of the firm is to conduct your trades. Some brokers are experienced in day trading than others.

Real-time Market Information

- Market news and data are essential when it comes to day trading.

- This information allows you to customize your strategies accordingly.

Monitors

Most computers have a capability that enables them to connect to more than one monitor.

Classes

You must train some of the strategies you need to succeed in the business.

Charting Software

The software helps you identify the right opportunities by indicating when and how you should start and close positions. They always display the necessary patterns required to estimate future changes in stock prices.

How to Choose Day Trading Charts

- Responsiveness

- Cost

- Stability

- Type of Indicators

- User-friendly

CHAPTER 12:

The Dos and Don'ts of Day Trading

D ay trading is a business that you can set up fast. The very first step is to define if you are a full-time or part-time day trader. The first rule of a trading business is that you should not trade with the money that, if lost, is likely to dent your lifestyle. This money, in the world of trading, is known as 'scarred money.' When you are trading with scarred money, fear comes to haunt your decisions, and you lose more often a winning bet. You will be making the worst possible trading choices and lose money in the end.

Do's

The basic thing is to be persistent in your approach. You should keep going even amid adversity. No one masters anything from the first attempt. You need time to build and polish your skills. You usually are pretty bad at first, but you learn to make it right over time because you have an urge buried down in your heart to make it better.

Don't try to give up on a couple of failed trades. You may lose some part of your capital while you desperately attempt to bag profits from a trade. If you have failed, you must push past this pain and keep your gaze fixed at the horizon. You must keep in mind the final destination. Only then can you get over the desperation and the frustration.

When you make up your mind about making a career out of day trading, you should create a tangible and practical plan that you must strictly follow. Every business demands a strategic plan that you must build and evolve along the way. A good plan should contain all aspects of your trading strategy. Without a solid plan, you are not trading but gambling. So, don't just gamble. Follow set rules. Your plan may contain the timing of your trade, the amount of initial investment, the companies you want to invest in, the timing you want to hold a stock, and the time you will have to invest in studying technical reports, charts, and volumes of a given stock.

Do prepare a checklist. A checklist usually is as much important as a trading plan. You need to include your trading rules in the list. You should be satisfied with the checklist before you enter a trade. For example, you can decide how much leverage you need to take and the risk-reward ratio. Going through the checklist each time you make a new trade cuts down your chance of making any kind of silly beginner-level mistakes. Once you have done trading for a couple of months, all the checklist points will be fed in your brain, and you will not need them anymore.

You should follow a strict routine. Day trading is not like a job or physical business that binds you for a set period. Trading is a lonely endeavor, and some of you may struggle after finding themselves in a new situation in which they are not under the watch of any kind and are not being instructed on what to do. It is you who have to make decisions and shape your future. Therefore, you must have a routine. It will be risky for your capital and your business if you take long breaks from work during active trading hours. You may miss out on high-probability opportunities. If you have set up a daily routine by defining your goals, you can remain on track and build a successful career as an independent trader.

Don'ts

The very first don'ts of day trading is emotional instability. If you feel that you lose emotional control easily and get angry or overly happy each time you try to make money, you will not follow the recipe to success. A forex trader or stock trader cannot be angry or extremely happy. The best traders across the world are the ones who can part their emotions from trading.

If a person pays heed to rumors around him, the best method to deal with him is to ignore him. You will not like to talk to someone who always lends his ear to rumors about politics or other national issues. The same is true in the world of trading as well. You cannot listen to rumors and act on them.

Remember that you don't need to listen to rumors no matter whatever the scenario is. You must do in-depth research before you act on a rumor.

You should not isolate yourself from others. It is very natural for you to do so because it is the need for this business. There are two reasons as to why isolation happens in the first place. Day traders have to work from home and focus on the latest analysis coming from different sources. The concentration and amount of study involved in its demand that you work in isolation.

Try to focus on teaming up with a group of professional traders who will support each other throughout the busy day. You can sense how other traders are approaching their business and solve the problems that arise over the day.

Chapter Summary

The very first step in day trading is to define if you are a full-time or part-time day trader.

Do's

- Be persistent in your approach.

- Don't try to give up on a couple of failed trades.

- Create a tangible and practical plan that you must strictly follow

- Do prepare a checklist

- Follow a strict routine

Don'ts

- The very first don'ts of day trading is emotional instability

- Do not deal with rumors

- Do not isolate yourself from others

Conclusion

D ay traders involved in the buying and selling of securities are fully investing in this trading activity with multiple learning sources, learning time, and good capital often end up being so successful. Being successful in day trading means acquiring a large portion of profits.

Being a day trader does not come out naturally; a specific personality and traits are duly required. Below are some characteristics of a day trader:

Disciplined

This is a major trait that day traders need to input. Day traders should always be disciplined to remain input when no opportunities emerge and act so fast when opportunities are available. Acting fast also includes strictly considering the step by step rules and obligations initially formed in their big plans.

Open-minded

Day trading is a learning kind of income-generating engagement, implying that there will be happy times and downfalls. Save yourself and learn from all that. Improve the happy times and completely discard the wrong downfall moves. Being exposed to the winnings and failures makes you open-minded, a master of all possible win moves.

A fan of technology

Day trading is carried out in various trading platforms and systems that a trader needs to be familiarized with. This should not scare you. Getting to know how they work does not, in any case, require you to be a computer whiz. Get to learn the basic moves and grow technologically with time.

Mentally tough

Losing market trades are constant; most successful traders will have losing trades every single day. They typically win slightly more times than they lose. Therefore, it is essential to stay focused and rational during a losing period and do not let in the basic fact that money has been lost too. Focus on the future day trading activities by implementing some strategies outlined in a big plan.

Independence

Independence is striving to build the toolbox that will forever lead you. Reading trading books, watching every video, interacting with one mentor after the other, can be a total miss. What if different books have one confusing point on a particular field? What is your YouTube subscriber who decides to quit vlogging? Always grasp the basics after in-depth research and day stay put. Dare to yourself that you've got you and get the large chunks of benefits. However, when you feel you are so lost, do not hesitate to get assistance. Most importantly, master and analyze successful moves and let them be a part of your big plan.

Patience

Good things do take quite some time. In every strategical move, you try to make, think about it carefully, but this should not make you paranoid. Act accordingly with many disciplines to reduce the number of losses likely to be incurred during various day trading activities.

Also, a patient day trader is a learning day trader. Day trading is not going to be easy at first, but with time, when you are equipped with lots of skills and experience, things are expected to flow smoothly. Hey, be patient.

Future-oriented

Getting stuck in the past makes you much of a prisoner. Forward-thinking lets you see the possible moves and gives you the final air when the next trading activity will occur considering the set protocols in the day trader's plan. Being future-oriented incites forward-thinking, which involves rational thinking and knowing your next possible moves after a considerate examination. Being future-oriented hastens and simplifies the day trading operation moves, and the chances are that they will be successful.

Financial freedom

Day trading does not necessarily require you to be a tycoon, but you must have a specific amount of money that has been precisely selected to begin day trading. Remember, first times are always won or lose situations; however, as you continue to learn and grow, this set of money can be lost.

Enthusiasm

High interest in something is a pending successful goal. A great enthusiastic inclination to stocks, securities, commodities, markets, and business gives you the thirst to learn and master what day trading is all about. These are signs of a future successful day trader.

Experience and familiarity

Experience comes with pretty much of downfall lessons and learning. Expose yourself to different learning sources and master every profitable move during day trading to squeeze the best out of that. Getting the trading platforms' experience and familiarity and various strategies needed to be successful at day trading is worthwhile.

Final Word

Thank you for reading! The world of day trading is indeed a challenging one. Day traders are continuously bombarded by news, fundamental market data, rumors, and trading programs that create numerous opportunities. These opportunities are fraught with risk. Given the lightning speed of news delivery via the Internet and the ability to execute trading orders instantly, day trading opportunities are more plentiful than ever.

The risks, as well as the opportunities, demand knowledge, structure, discipline, and profitable methodologies. Key trading tools for success and clear and effective risk management and profit-maximizing strategy form the essential underpinnings of a profitable day trading program. The systems and methods must be put into practice with consistency, organization, and persistence. In short, there is no substitute for practice

There are five key areas to success as a day trader.

Methodology: There are several day-trading methods. The goal is to give a step-by-step procedure by which day trades can be implemented, executed, and managed from the standpoint of risk and reward. The less objective your methods are, the less likely you will be to succeed.

Structure: The essential of all-day trades is a solid structure within which the decision-making process operates. Without a trading model, the odds are that you will lose money, whether you are a day trader or a position trader.

Focus: Most day, traders believe that more is better when it comes to trading. They feel that they must try to take advantage of every price swing or every opportunity that comes their way. In attempting to actualize this feeling, they tend to become scattered in their attention and frequently miss changes in their indicators, or their error rate increases. I believe that in day trading, less is more. It is much better off focusing on a few markets rather than many and a few opportunities rather than many.

Time frame: The time frame in which you operate as a day trader is also critically important. As a day trader, you will be presented with numerous opportunities in numerous of these frames. You need to think and decide if you want to trade in the five-minute, ten-minute, thirty-minute, sixty-minute, or other time frames. Different time frames will give different signals. What may be a buying opportunity in the thirty-minute time frame may be a selling opportunity in the ten-minute time frame. The more time frames you use in your work, the more confused you will become. The one that gets you into a day trade should be the time frame that gets you out of a day trade. Mixing them does not lead to clarity; rather, it is the first step to confusion. Confusion will lead to losses.

Profit-maximizing strategy: You must have and use a profit-maximizing strategy for all of your day trades. Eighty percent to 90 percent of your money will be made on 10 percent to 20 percent of your trades as a day trader. Without the large winning trades, your success as a day trader will be limited. You will generate many small profits, which will be balanced by the cost of commissions and small losses. Unless you have a clear and concise method for maximizing profits, your efforts as a day trader will not be rewarded.

Happy trading!